MILITARY SLANG

Abson Books London
First published October 2006
4th impression September 2011
© Fred Holcroft
Cover design Chris Bird

Printed by Gutenberg Press, Malta
ISBN 978 0 902920 92 7

MILITARY SLANG

compiled by Lee Pemberton

ABSON
BOOKS
LONDON
5 Sidney Square London E1 2EY
Tel 020 7790 4737 Fax 020 7790 7346
email absonbooks@aol.com | web www.absonbooks.co.uk

INTRODUCTION

All enclosed and self-disciplined societies develop their own customs and traditions, often including a highly individual slang language. One tends to think in particular of the criminal fraternity, the gay scene and the schoolyard. The military, with their need for quick identification and rapid response, coupled in many cases with their desire for complete secrecy, are another example. All branches of the services, with some overlapping, have evolved their own unique slang language.

The Royal Navy, the senior service, has had longest to create its own vernacular, but while it loves to hang on to its proud traditions, the transition from sail to more modern power has left much of the terminology obsolete. However, many naval phrases have entered everyday life such as *to miss the boat, show a leg, know the ropes, sail close to the wind, above board,* etc.

The British Army's long service in India has led to the absorption into its vocabulary of native words from that continent, many of which have been further absorbed by the home civilian population.

The Royal Air Force, although the youngest of the services, is the most highly developed technically, with a need for simple words to replace complicated terminology.

The Royal Marines, a small proud elite and highly proficient service, have probably coined more slang for its size than the rest put together.

During the Cold War, the British and American forces developed an overlapping slang (though not unified) for use against a common foe but the solo involvement of the Americans in Vietnam brought about a change which is all but incomprehensible to their allies and which is being re-learned in the Gulf. Today, the vast bulk of the military slang which exists is of American origin but the small, professional, all-regular British forces possess a unique patter. Many words are derogatory – especially when relating to one of the other services – and given the male-dominated origin from which they evolved, many are vulgar and have a sexual nature.

Here are over 300 words to give you a flavour of military slang.

ABBREVIATIONS

Royal Navy   (RN)
Royal Marines   (RM)
Royal Air Force   (RAF)

A

above board	honest	RM
ack ack	anti-aircraft fire	ARMY
addlings	back pay accumulated on voyage	RN
admiral's mate	know all	RN
adrift	misplaced	RN
adult	senior officer	RN
aimer	driver	RM
Ali Barba	Iraqi looter	ARMY
amen wallah	chaplain	ARMY
angels	height in thousands of feet	RAF
angel track	armoured personnel carrier used as an ambulance	ARMY
Andy Capp's Commandos	Army Catering Corp – reputed to have killed more men than the rest of the British army	ARMY

7

arsy tarsy	aircrew reception centre	RAF
ash can	depth charge	RN

B

badged	accepted into Special Forces	ARMY
back to the taxpayers	wrecked aircraft	RAF
bag off	have sex	RM
bag rat	packed lunch	RM
bag shanty	brothel	ARMY
balbo	large formation of aircraft	RAF
bandit	enemy aircraft	RAF
bale out	abandon plane by parachute – now means to leave a place	RAF
bang box	gun turret	RM
bang on	on target – now means correct	RAF
barn	aircraft hangar	RAF

barnacle	officer in a soft job	RN
basha	improvised shelter	ARMY
bat turn	fast, tight manoeuvre	RAF
beached	retired	RN
beaded	worried	ARMY
beat up	fly low over airfield	RAF
beef bayonet	penis	RM
biff chit	sick note	ARMY
bimble	stroll	ARMY
bind	unexpected obstruction – now means nuisance	ARMY
bin liner job	ugly woman	RM
bite	fool someone into doing something stupid	RM
black nasty	adhesive tape	ARMY
blades	SAS personnel	ARMY
blat	small arms fire	ARMY

black	bad	RAF
bleeps	Royal Signals personnel	ARMY
blighty	home	ARMY
blitz	large formation of enemy aircraft	RAF
blue jobs	RAF personnel	ARMY
blue on blue	friendly fire	ARMY
BOBFOC	she's got the Body Of Baywatch/ Face Off Crimewatch	ARMY
bogey	unidentified enemy aircraft	RAF
bondhook	rifle	ARMY
bogging	dirty	ARMY
bootnecks	Royal Marines personnel	ARMY
bowser	fuel truck	RAF
brass/brasshat	senior officer	ARMY
Bravo Zulu	well done	ARMY

brew	tea (verb or noun)	ARMY
brolly	parachute	RAF
brown job	army personnel	RAF
browned off/ brassed off	bored	ALL
Brylcream boys	RAF personnel (obsolete)	ARMY
bull	seemingly unnecessary formalities and work	ALL
buttoned up	job well done	RAF

C

cabbage commando	chef	ARMY
cabbage head	Royal Marine personnel	ARMY
cabbage suit	combat suit	RAF
cabin	sleep	ARMY

cake and arse party	not very good – any bad situation	RN
can	Saracen armoured personnel carrier	ARMY
can spanner	tin opener	RM
catch a packet	hit by enemy fire	RAF
catshoot	catapult-assisted carrier takeoff	RN
char	tea	ARMY
check six	watch out behind	RAF
chins	bad luck	RM
chinstraps	knackered/tired	RM
choker	fed up	ARMY
chota wallah	small	ARMY
chop-chop	more quickly	ALL
chunky	Pioneer	ARMY
clapped out	anything nearing the end of its useful life – machinery or people	ARMY

clobber	clothing and equipment	ARMY
cock up	something gone badly wrong	ARMY
college	prison	ARMY
compo	composition rations	ARMY
corkscrew	evasive manoeuvre	RAF
crabbing	flying low over water	RAF
crash out	go to sleep after hard duty	ARMY
creamy	top flying instructor	RAF
crummy	no good	ARMY
cushy	easy	ARMY
custard	rifle	ARMY

daisy chaining	sex with several ladies consecutively	ARMY
darky	radio signals to lost aircraft	RAF
dekko	look – take a dekko	ARMY

devil dodger	chaplin	RM
dhobi	washing	ARMY
dhobi dust	washing powder	ARMY
dhobi marks	rank badges	RM
dhobi rash	irritation from clothing not rinsed properly	ARMY
dhobi run	trip to the launderette	ARMY
dhobi wallah	laundry personnel	ARMY
dicked	ordered to do unpopular duty	ARMY
dicky seat	second pilot's seat	RAF
diggers	knife fork spoon	ARMY
dig out	help yourself/make an effort	RM
dipped	missed out on something	ARMY
ditch	land aircraft in the sea	RAF
do a never	avoid work	ARMY

dockyard omelette	vomit	RM
dog fight	aerial combat	RAF
doggo	hidden	ARMY
dolly mixture	alternative round of high explosive and white phosphorous	ARMY
doofer	anything that fits	RM
doss	sleep	ARMY
doss bag	sleeping bag	ARMY
double bagger	very ugly woman	RM
Dreadnought	contraceptive	RN
drink	sea	RAF
drip/dripping tap	grumble incessantly	RN
dud	counterfeit/bad weather	RAF
duff	false (particularly information)	ARMY
duffer	incompetent (especially officers)	ARMY

E

egg banjo	fried egg sandwich	ARMY
eggo	bald	ARMY
erks	ground crew	RAF
essence	attractive woman	RM

F

fag	cigarette	ARMY
fangs out	aircraft ready for action	RAF
fanny	kettle	RN
fat Albert	Hercules troop transport plane	ARMY
fighting order	knife fork spoon	ARMY
fish	torpedo	RN

fish-heads	navy personnel	RAF
flak	anti-aircraft fire	ALL
flannel	boast	RN
flat hatting	unauthorised low flying	RAF
flange	good looking female	RM
fleabag	sleeping bag	ARMY
floaters	sausages	RN
flog the dolphin	tell a lie	RN
free the slide	pass the butter	RM
full screw	corporal	ARMY

gam	hammock	RN
gardening	mine-laying at sea	RAF

gash	a multi-purpose word used in different situations:	
	free *I got it gash*	ARMY
	rubbish *this is gash*	ARMY
	stingy *lend me a quid, you gash*	ARMY
gat	weapon	ARMY
gen	information	ALL
george	automatic pilot	RAF
get aft	promoted officer from the ranks	RN
get some in	experience needed	ARMY
glasshouse	military prison	ARMY
glitter	marmalade	ALL
gobbler's gulch	homosexual hangout	RM
goffer	non-alcoholic drink	RM
gomer	dogfight opponent	RAF
gong	medal	ALL

gonk	sleep	RM
gonkbag	sleeping bag	ARMY
goolies	testicles	ARMY
goolie chit	paper in English and Arabic promising monetary reward for return of shot down pilot and not just his testicles	RAF
graft	work	ALL
green	permission to take off	RAF
greenhouse	cockpit cover	RAF
gremlin	machine malfunction where the cause cannot be located	ARMY
griff	information	RN
grollies	underwear	ARMY
growler	NAAFI pie	ARMY

H

halo	high altitude, low opening – a dangerous parachute jump	ARMY
hang on the slack	wait for something to happen	RN
harpooned	captured	ARMY
hedgehopping	low flying	RAF
hockey	assault rifle made by Heckler and Koch	ARMY
hoist in	accept a suggestion	RN
horse box	sergeant's mess	RM

I

icers	very cold	RM
in the rattle	in trouble	RM

J

jack	selfish	ARMY
jankers	time served in military prison	ARMY
jarhead	new recruit	ARMY
jenny spinner	cockroach	RN
jimpy	general purpose machine gun	ARMY
jink	aircraft evasive action	RAF
jinglies	locally employed Iraqis – who pick up spent cartridges and smelt them down	ALL
joe	senior officer	RM
juice	aviation fuel	RAF

K

kaput	broken	ARMY
kebabside	posted to Iraq	ARMY

killik	leading hand	RN
kip	sleep	ARMY
kite	aircraft	RAF
KitKat arse	after sitting still for hours	ARMY
know the ropes	experienced	RN
kye	hot cocoa	RN

L

lammy	duffle coat	RN
lance jack	lance corporal	ARMY
lid	helmet	ARMY
loadie	crewman	RAF
loot	personal belongings	ARMY
lousy	no good	ARMY
lumpy jumper	female soldier	ARMY
luncheon trumpet	penis	ARMY

M

Mae West	inflatable life jacket	ALL
maggot	sleeping bag	ARMY
mahogany Spitfire	desk	RAF
make and mend	spare time/early finish	RN
manky	dirty, smelly	ARMY
milk run	routine mission	RAF
miss the boat	late	RN
monkeys	Royal Military Police	ARMY
monkey's wedding	bad smell	RN
muster	sea sick	RN

N

nadged	damaged	ARMY
neaters	undiluted rum	RN
nod	new recruit	RM
noddy suit	nuclear, chemical, biological warfare protective suit	ARMY
no load	useless personnel	ARMY

O

odd bod	spare man	ARMY
oily	cigarette – cockney slang: *oily rag/fag*	ARMY
old sweat	veteran	ALL
old man	commanding officer – male or female	ALL
one up	sole surveillance	ARMY
over the wall	serving a sentence in detention	ARMY

P

padlocked	enemy aircraft fixed in sights	RAF
pash	girlfriend	RM
pear shaped	badly wrong	ALL
peel off	break formation	RAF
penguin	ground crew/paratrooper – has wings, can't fly	RAF
periscope depth	half asleep	RN
piece of cake	easy	RAF
pile up points	curry favour with superiors	RN
pinged	picked for disagreeable duty	ARMY
planters	smart clothes	ARMY
platform four	failed SAS selection	ARMY
play pussy	hide in the clouds	RAF

plug away	keep firing	ARMY
pongo	army personnel	RN/RAF
poodle fakir	officer spending too much time inpolite female society	ARMY
pop wallah	teetotal	ARMY
pork sword	penis	ARMY
prang	aircraft crash – usually on landing	RAF
proffing	suspect acquisition of goods, usually of government origin	ARMY
pukka	genuine	ALL
pulpit	cockpit	RAF
pundit	flashing light to assist navigation	RAF

quaffer	posh officer	RM
Queens	truth – *It's Queens honest*	ARMY

R

rabbits	items smuggled ashore	RN
rat arsed	drunk	ARMY
rattle	trouble	RN
redcap	Royal Military Police personnel	ARMY
retread	late entry officer	ARMY
rig	uniform	RN
ring the bell	good results	RAF
rock ape	stationed on Gibraltar	ARMY
rookie	new recruit	ARMY
ropy	unsatisfactory	ARMY
rotty botty	diahorrea	ARMY
roughers	stormy weather	RM
rub	loan – usually financial	RN
rupert	recently qualified junior officer	ARMY

S

sad on	miserable – *he's got a sad on*	ARMY
sail close to the wind	take risks	RN
salvo	bombs released simultaneously	RAF
scaly	signaller	ARMY
scramble	get airborne ASAP	RAF
scran	food	ARMY
screaming downhill	power drive	RAF
sea legs	steady once the ship puts to sea	RN
shiny arse	clerk	ALL
shellback	sailor who has crossed the Equator	RN
shreddies	underwear	ARMY
shonky	mean	RN
shooting a line	exaggerating – usually about oneself	ARMY

skivvies	underwear	ARMY
sky pilot	chaplain	ARMY
slack bladder	lazy	ARMY
smoker	get together – *let's have a smoker*	ARMY
smudge	sub-machine gun	ARMY
SNAFU	Situation Normal, All Fucked Up	ARMY
snake about	aerobatics	RAF
snapper	homosexual	ARMY
snottie	midshipman	RN
snowdrop	RAF Military Police personnel	RAF
sooner	avoids work	ARMY
space cadet	not with it	ARMY
spammed	involuntarily volunteered	ARMY
sparks	radio operator	RN
sparrow's fart	early start	ARMY

sprog	young recruit	ALL
squaddie	private soldier	ARMY
squared away	ready for inspection	RN
squirt	short, sharp burst of fire	ARMY
stag	guard duty	ARMY
stick	bombs released at intervals	RAF
stonk	mortar attack	ARMY
stonking	excellent	ARMY
stooging	aimless flying	RAF
swallow the anchor	leave the navy	RN
synthetic	ground training	RAF

tab	quick march	ARMY
tailend charlie	rear gunner	RAF

tally	false name	RN
tear off a strip	reprimand	ARMY
top off	refuel	ARMY
turdies	portaloos	ALL

U

unhook	borrow without owner's permission	ARMY
up and downer	argument, possibly a fight	ARMY
up the line	on leave	ARMY

V

vegetables	magnetic mines	RAF

W

warm the bell	arrive early for duty	ARMY
wazz	urinate	ARMY
weave	aircraft manoeuvre	RAF
wellies from the Queen	free condoms issued overseas	RM
wet/wet behind the ears	inexperienced	ARMY
Whiskey Tango Foxtrot	What The Fuck	RAF
Willy Wonka	Chinook helicopter	ARMY
winger	close friend – but *do a winger* means *pull a fast one* or *betray a friend*	ARMY
wizard	excellent – now largely obsolete	RAF

Y

yaffle	eat	RM
yaffle irons	knives forks spoons	RM
yodel in a bucket	vomit	RM
yo yo	young officer in training	RM
yomp	cross-country march in full kit	RM

Z

zap	shoot	ALL
zoombag	flight suit	RAF
Zulu	Greenwich meantime	RM

OTHER TITLES AVAILABLE

Language Glossaries

American English/English American
Australian English/English Australian
Irish English/English Irish
Gay Slang
Geordie English
Lancashire English
Rhyming Cockney Slang
Scouse English
Yiddish English/English Yiddish
Yiddish English/English Yiddish
Yorkshire English

Prison Slang
Hip Hop English
Rude Rhyming Slang
Military Slang
Home Counties English
Playground Slang
Cumbrian English
West Country English
Police Slang
London Taxi Driver Slang

History
The Death of Kings
(A medical history of the Kings & Queens of England)

Who's Buried Where? -
Discover where Royalty, the famous & infamous are buried

Literary Quiz & Puzzle Books
Jane Austen	Gilbert & Sullivan
Brontë Sisters	Thomas Hardy
Charles Dickens	Sherlock Holmes
	Shakespeare

USE THIS FOR YOUR OWN MILITARY SLANG:
